LIVING BEHIND THE MASK

2020 a Year Like No Other

Tammie R Williams

LIVING BEHIND THE MASK
2020 a Year Like No Other
Copyright © 2021 by Tammie R Williams

All rights reserved. No part of this publication may be reproduced, distributed, or transmitted in any form or by any means, including photocopying, recording, or other electronic or mechanical methods, without the prior written permission of the publisher or author, except in the case of brief quotations embodied in critical reviews and certain other noncommercial uses permitted by copyright law.

Although every precaution has been taken to verify the accuracy of the information contained herein, the author and publisher assume no responsibility for any errors or omissions. No liability is assumed for damages that may result from the use of information contained within.

Library of Congress Control Number: 2021919283
ISBN-13: Paperback: 978-1-64749-600-5
          Epub: 978-1-64749-601-2

Printed in the United States of America

GoToPublish LLC
1-888-337-1724
www.gotopublish.com
info@gotopublish.com

Contents

Introduction	v
Living Behind the Mask 2020: A Year Like No Other	1
December 26, 2019	5
GOD Is Never Surprised	8
GOD Has Walked Where I Am	14
Time to be Uncomfortably Honest	19
Not Sure Where This Is Going	24
What Am I to Do with That?	26
Living Behind the Mask	28
This Isn't It	31
September 19, 2017	33
Coming to a Close	35
So...Now What?	37
No Longer My Reference Point	41
Where Am I Now?	43

A Thanks to my family and friends who have walked with me on this path during the year of unknowns. Thanks for your constant love and reminders of CHRIST's goodness, HIS faithfulness, and HIS trustworthiness. You truly loved me like CHRIST."The King will reply,"Truly I tell you whatever you did for one of the least if these brothers and sisters of mine, you did for me.""Matthew 25:40 NIV

INTRODUCTION

For most, the ending of one year into another brings the opportunity for closure and new beginnings. Every New Year's Eve allows us to let go of the disappointments and unfinished projects or business and gives us permission to move forward with the hope of doing things better than we have before—to improve on the lessons we learned in the previous and to actually make those changes we have been promising to make each year as one year ends and another "new" year begins. The New Year seems to bring a hope of a newness to the life we live. It brings a freshness to the normal and an opportunity to start again.

Who knew, when most were celebrating December 31, 2019, the ushering in of the new year of 2020, the rumors of some virus that had begun someplace in the world and would impact a year, as well as our future, in the way it has. Little did the world know that 1/6th of the way into 2020 the year we had expected to be was going to be one like no other. It became the year of unknowns because of the impact of COVID-19 worldwide. How long would the world be shut down? When would schools reopen or sporting events resume? Will we be living behind mask indefinitely? These and so many other unanswered questions filled the days of 2020 while we all adjusted to what we hoped would not become our new normal. This was 2020 for all, a year of unknowns.

Personally, the year 2020 was a year like no other not because of the unknowns caused by the pandemic but because 2019 ended in a way I was not expecting. In 2020, I was asked to answer the question "if your life looks much differently than what you expected it to look, are you and JESUS still good?" Through the unknowns of 2020, the depth of GOD's promises of HIS goodness trustworthiness and faithfulness became known in a different way than I had known before. What follows is my journey of living behind the mask, 2020 a year like no other.

LIVING BEHIND THE MASK 2020: A YEAR LIKE NO OTHER

Living behind the mask? Wow, when I first had these thoughts mid-January 2020, I did not have any clue how apropos this would be for the actual year of 2020. Now that we are eight months into the year and about five to six months into this thing called the pandemic, the Covid-19 pandemic, we literally are all living behind a mask. Now I am not going to promise my thoughts will have any type of chronological timeline. These are just thoughts that I have had since a significant date in my life, which was December 26, 2019. The significance of that date will be explained here in a moment. If you have ever read any of my thoughts I have written, you know my thoughts are all pretty random. They don't really have a flow, they don't really have a—let's say—a systematic way of coming out. They literally are pretty much all over the place, but through God's wisdom and God's Holy Spirit, I hope these thoughts are woven together in a way that will enable you to benefit from reading them. If it's not a direct benefit to you, maybe you will be given some insight or something you can share with someone else so they can benefit from these random thoughts that have come to me through experiences over the last eight months of 2020.

In 2 Corinthians 1:3–7 (MSG), it says, "All praise to the God and Father of our Master, Jesus the Messiah! Father of all mercy! God of all healing counsel! He comes alongside us when we go through hard times, and before you know it, he brings us alongside someone else who is going through hard times so that we can be there for that person just as God was there for us. We have plenty of hard times that come from following the Messiah, but no more so than the good times of his healing comfort—we get a full measure of that, too. When we suffer for Jesus, it works out for your healing and salvation. If we are treated well, given a helping hand and encouraging word, that also works to your benefit, spurring you on, face forward, unflinching. Your hard times are also our hard times. When we see that you're just as willing to endure the hard times as to enjoy the good times, we know you're going to make it, no doubt about it."

The life experiences we go through with Christ by our side, when we lean in and we push into the faithfulness of Christ and into our relationship with Christ, we are equipped to be able to benefit others, who are experiencing similar situations, much like I have over the last eight months. Because of the path I have been on, unfortunately, I now have knowledge and understanding that I wish I didn't have. That knowledge of knowing has come from life experiences that I have gained yet I wish I hadn't gained. Which I refer to now as, unfortunate opportunities, meaning opportunities that have come only because of an unfortunate experience. Up until that day in December of 2019, I didn't have the experience and understanding mentioned because I had never had the unfortunate opportunity (yes, it is an opportunity even though it has been the toughest opportunity to date that I have been given) to experience life in a way as I have. How does this, which seems to be opposite thoughts, come together? It is unfortunate that I had to walk through these experiences to gain the understanding I now have. Understanding, which I thought I had but actually didn't, I have now gained because of where I have walked the last eight months.

I thought I understood what it meant to grieve. I thought I knew what it meant when someone's life was suddenly shattered. I thought I understood what it meant to have to have faith to get one through a trial. I had no clue life could become so unstable this side of eternity that I would be shaken to the core of my very being. But now I, unfortunately, really know what I thought I already did.

I now have the opportunity because of the experience and the understanding I have gained through this most difficult time, to be a blessing and a benefit to others because of these very experiences. My understanding has been deepened. My wisdom has been broadened. I now understand things that I did not and never wanted to really have to understand. I have discovered, it is much easier to be strong and stable for someone else when their life is rocked and experiencing the hard and difficult, as long as my life is going along as I expected. I have found I was more than able to use my experiences to help others through their trials, but what about now when my experiences have become hard? What about when my experiences have become opportunities for my understanding to be deepened? It has caused growth in wisdom and understanding that I, quite honestly, now know I never really desired because as I now know having this depth of understanding requires a lot of hardship for it to be gained. What if GOD asks you to walk on a path that you have no desire to walk but HE promises to never leave you or forsake you, which is guaranteed in HIS HOLY WORD numerous times? HE also promises HE will be glorified and others will be benefitted as mentioned in the verse above. That is where I have been asked to walk, not only these past eight months but from here on.

Hopefully through my ramblings that are to follow you will be encouraged to not worry about your trustworthiness but will become secure in HIS trustworthiness. You will be less concerned about being faithful but will come to know CHRIST's faithfulness. My prayer is you will truly come to be secure in knowing "you can do all things through CHRIST who strengthens you" not because of what you possess but because of WHO possesses you.

DECEMBER 26, 2019

You know what, to bring this into this conversation, I am going to share something I wrote April 3, 2020, in the midst of the beginning of the world shutting down. (Remember I warned you these thoughts will not follow a timeline.) So here goes.

Hand over the fear of the unknown into the hands of the ALL knowing. My unknown began December 26, 2019, when Ted (my husband) woke me and said, "I need to go to the emergency room." The unknown began immediately because he had never said those words to me before. On December 31, 2019, the door to the unknown flew open wider than I knew it could as Ted got to walk into the perfect presence of Christ. While joyful for him, the girls—Bridget, Andrea, Kara—and I were left not just standing at the door of the unknown but we now had to walk through it.

I have heard that the first days after someone leaves this earth becomes a blur for those still on earth. Honestly, I wish that was true, but I remember every detail of almost every day since December 26th. It is like my brain is on deep record and every moment is there to be replayed at any point in time, which is a constant reminder of this unknown I am walking in.

During these last thirteen weeks since walking through that door of unknown, the LORD has reminded me time and time again, "Tammie, yes, you are walking in the unknown, but trust ME who is not surprised. I am never in the unknown because I am the ALL knowing. I could give you the details and understanding of my perfect plan I have for you and the girls, but I don't want to provide anything that would cause you to be less dependent on ME your heavenly FATHER. Just know I am never surprised by the things of this world. I see all. I know all. My heart grieves for the hurt and pain that is present in my creation. But MY promise to renew all into perfection through MY SON is still, my, promise. I am trustworthy. I am faithful and I am not surprised. Let me comfort you in this unknown because I am the ALL knowing."

I share this because now the entire world seems to be in the unknown. What we had become comfortable with, in knowing what to expect each day, has been totally flipped, twisted, and wrecked—whatever word one wants to use to describe this unknown. Just know GOD is not surprised. HIS promise HE made to Abraham has come to be through CHRIST. HIS promise through CHRIST to bring us into HIS perfect eternity is still to come. So as much as the world wants us to believe we are living in times of unknown and uncertainty, know that GOD is reminding us that we actually do know what is to come. Eternity with Him! Walk with HIM! Be blessed.

Okay, so now you know that I lost my husband, Ted. Wait! I don't want to say lost because I know where he is. Ted went to walk with Jesus on December 31, 2019, and I'll discuss those five days later. For now, let's say, yeah that was a life-changing event I was not prepared for. We had just buried his dad two months earlier, and his dad was ninety-seven years old who actually drove the day he had his stroke. This literally was something that we had not prepared ourselves for. As people said, "Williams do not die in their 60s." I wish I could say that now, eight months later, my first thought of every morning wasn't "did that really happen?" But it still is. I don't know what stage the textbook would tell me I am in, where I would fall on the grief chart.

Wherever I am I know that CHRIST is with me, and I now understand on a much deeper level what Paul meant in Philippians 4:11-13: "I am not saying this because I am in need, for I have learned to be content whatever the circumstances. I know what it is to be in need, and I know what it is to have plenty. I have learned the secret of being content in any and every situation, whether well fed or hungry, whether living in plenty or in want. I can do all this through him who gives me strength." Even if you find yourself on a road you would never have picked for yourself, CHRIST is enough.

GOD IS NEVER SURPRISED

Am I still dealing with the shock and the disbelief in how those five days changed my earthly life? Yes, unfortunately, I have also come to realize how the LORD had been preparing me for those five days as well as the days that have followed.

To explain what I mean by GOD has been preparing me, I have to go back to June of 2018. During the summer of 2018, I was working at K-Kauai, the family camp of Kanakuk Ministries. I was talking to a young lady (great conversation by the way) when she said her only desire was to be a mom and a wife. Before I knew it, I asked her, "But what if that doesn't happen? Are you and Jesus still good?" I had never asked anyone that question (even myself). She looked at me and said, "Well, that's not something I have to worry about because God gave me these desires, therefore, he's going to make it come true because he gives you the desires of your heart." Great example of the ways we tend to take scripture out of context. Anyway, I said again, "But if it doesn't happen, are you and JESUS still good?" She looked at me with a look of confusion like I don't get it and changed the conversation.

For the next year and a half that became a challenge question that I would ask people: if your life doesn't look the way you think it should, are you and JESUS still good? Meaning is your relationship built on who Jesus is, or who or what he does for you? In early October 2019 I was talking to my friend Kathi Hutton, who is the assistant campus minister at Midland where I was now teaching. I shared how that question had become my challenge question to others in conversations. Suddenly I sensed the Holy Spirit asking me, "What about you, Tammie, if your life doesn't look like you expect are you and I still good?" While the conversation was still going on, I became so uncomfortable and don't remember anything else that was said. At the moment my focus was on what I knew my answer was, "Lord, please don't ask me that question. I know what I want and hope my answer would be, but I am honestly afraid to know."

Now let me say it isn't like my life hasn't had challenges and that I haven't had difficult times that I had to walk through. But I also knew a lot of those difficult times I had contributed too by choices I made growing up. There also had been difficult times—losing my parents and a precious niece (which by the way was the most difficult trial up to this point)—but I knew when this question was asked, "if your life doesn't look how you expect it to look are you and I still good?" it meant something different than I had ever experienced. It meant that whether I wanted to know or not, I was going to find out my answer to that question.

Looking back now I realize how that moment in the halls of Midland Christian High School the Lord was beginning to prepare me for what was to come. Many times, the Lord is equipping us for what's ahead through our day-by-day moments, and because we are so caught up in the day's moments, we are unaware of how these moments will be used for what is ahead. "Now may the God of peace—who brought up from the dead our Lord Jesus, the great Shepherd of the sheep, and ratified an eternal covenant with his blood—may he equip you with all you need for doing his will. May he produce in you, through the power of Jesus Christ, every good thing that is pleasing to him. All glory to him forever and ever! Amen" (Hebrews 13:20-21, NLT)

So began the daily conversation within myself where I was asked my own challenge question that I had meant only for others. From that day in the halls of Midland Christian High School, I began each knowing that at some point I was going to be asked to walk in a way that would be different than anything I had yet experienced or had anticipated. I was going to have to answer the question. "If your life doesn't look like you expect it to look, are you and I (JESUS) still good?" I didn't share with anyone what was going except with CHRIST. Most of the time it was me asking, "Lord, what is it? What is ahead of me that is going to force me to answer that question up to now I thought was so cool to ask of someone? Please, Lord, change whatever is ahead, not because I don't have faith in You to see me through but I don't have faith in myself to walk through this unexpected in a manner that will bring glory to You and benefit others. I don't trust myself, Lord."

To which He gently reminded me, "I never wanted you to trust yourself or in your faith. My Faithfulness I give to my children is where you are to trust. I am trustworthy and I am faithful. Remember numerous times in my Word I have promised to never leave you or forsake my children. You are my child and that promise is for you as well. I never said your faith had to be big only the size of a mustard seed. I will see you through what is ahead. You will know my presence. I will be glorified and others will be benefitted. Trust Me I am faithful."

At this point, I tried to totally surrender because I knew something was going to rock my world and all I could do was wait for it to happen. I am not good at not having a plan, and this was something I could not plan for since I had no idea what "it" was to begin planning for it. I had no clue what was ahead nor could I anticipate when it was to come so I could be prepared to brace myself for it. These conversations continued with me praying and asking whatever and when it would be revealed, but my heavenly Father just kept responding with "I am faithful, I am trustworthy I will never leave you or forsake you. You are my child."

It was the first week of December when I had a dream that I did not like. It was one of those so real it is uncomfortable. But because of the last two months I also knew it was more than just a dream. In the dream it was after the first of the year and I was in Midland (where Ted and I lived), but Ted was not there. I was very upset and kept saying, "I can't do this. I don't want to this." Ugh! I thought, "No, Lord, please don't let this mean what my heart is telling me it does." I knew something was going to happen to Ted. I was praying it wasn't going to happen. So for the next three weeks, while Ted drove the dangerous roads of west Texas, I prayed and prayed, watched his location, was in constant contact with him making sure he was safe, and I prayed some more. When December 21st arrived, I relaxed and thought, "Thank you, Lord Jesus, for keeping Ted safe from these roads. Please remove these thoughts I am having that are bringing in fear that I know I don't need to have. Yes, you are trustworthy, You, are faithful."

With renewed hope, my worries had passed. We headed out of Midland to Woodward then on to Branson for Christmas break and to spend time with family. Not sure how to talk about the next five days leading up to December 26th, except they now are very special days in my heart—ones that seem like only moments that went by way too fast, leading into December 26 to December 31, which are days etched so deep into my soul that I am not sure the crevice will ever be filled again. Five days' memories that still seem to make time stand still yet I can recall almost minute by minute the moments of those 7200 minutes in my life that has challenged me in ways I didn't know I could be challenged but at the same time strengthened my hope in Christ.

In Lamentations 3:22-24 (NLT), it says "The faithful love of the Lord never ends! His mercies never cease. Great is his faithfulness; his mercies begin afresh each morning. I say to myself, "The Lord is my inheritance; therefore, I will hope in him!" 2019, when I read these verses, my thoughts were on God's goodness and His faithfulness and how He provides for us daily in the everyday things of this world. Since that day, these verses have taken on a depth that I hadn't considered until I was forced to consider. The Word of God is His promise to His children of His faithfulness, His goodness, and His love that goes so much deeper than we can even fathom. God's Word is not shallow, but it goes deep into the most dug out crevices of our lives to not just promise us of His goodness faithfulness and love but to reveal the truth of who He is.

In February, I received a text from our family friend Orson Sykes that actually expresses what I am trying to convey here.

Orson: I still really don't know what to say to you but I'm constantly praying for you. All I can do is declare God's truth and his truth is his word. I Love you and am here for you. He then sent these promises from GOD's Word: "Every single moment you are thinking of me! How precious and wonderful to consider that you cherish me constantly in your every thought! O God, your desires toward me are more than the grains of sand on every shore! When I awake each morning, you're still with me. There is no such thing as darkness with you. The night, to you, is as bright as the day; there's no difference between the two. You formed my innermost being, shaping my delicate inside and my intricate outside, and wove them all together in my mother's womb. I thank you, God, for making me so mysteriously complex! Everything you do is marvelously breathtaking. It simply amazes me to think about it! How thoroughly you know me, Lord! You even formed every bone in my body when you created me in the secret place, carefully, skillfully shaping me from nothing to something. You saw who you created me to be before I became me! Before I'd ever seen the light of day, the number of days you planned for me were already recorded in your book" (Psalms 139:12-18, TPT). Such perfect words I have held to many times during this season.

My response to Orson then for the beautiful promises from our Lord and Savior: I had no idea my life could be so wrecked but my faith in HIS faithfulness be so deepened at the same time. GOD is so, so, good even in the most difficult HE is faithful and loving and peace giving even when this world makes no sense. I know the verses you shared with me are so, so, true! Thanks so much for sharing them with me. In all things God is present. He is faithful. He is Good. Nothing of this world changes who God is. From the first breath He took to begin spinning this life in motion until Jesus returns to get His children. God remains the unmovable rock we are placed on. Shifting sands of this world does not cause Our Heavenly Father to shift on us. He is the same yesterday today and tomorrow. "Jesus Christ is the same yesterday, today, and forever. So, do not be attracted by strange, new ideas. Your strength comes from God's grace, not from rules about food, which don't help those who follow them" (Hebrews 13:8-9, NLT)

GOD HAS WALKED WHERE I AM

When Ted went to walk with Jesus, Jesus reminded me He has already been where I am headed, and He is now surrounding me with His protection love grace peace joy and comfort so I can walk in peace that doesn't make sense. As life has unfolded since that moment, God has continued to remind me of His presence in my current moment long before I arrived. Knowing God is and never was surprised by what has happened brings peace in the midst of the storm in a way that can only be explained by His goodness and extreme love He has for us His children. Through His Word, he promises to never leave us or forsake us, but He also promises He has been where we are.

> "The LORD is the one who goes ahead of you; He will be with you He will not fail you or forsake you. Do not fear or be dismayed."—Deuteronomy 31:8

> "The LORD your God who goes before you will Himself fight on your behalf."—Deuteronomy 1:30

"You go before me and follow me. You place your hand of blessing on my head."—Psalm 139:5 (NLT)

"For the LORD will go before you, And the God of Israel will be your rear guard."—Isaiah 52:12

"I will go before you and will level the mountains; I will break down gates of bronze and cut through bars of iron."—Isaiah 45:2

"To Him who led His people through the wilderness, For His lovingkindness is everlasting;"—Psalm 136:16.

These verses remind us that nothing surprises our Heavenly Father. His promise of always being with us and never leave us is so true as well as His promise of going before us. In the midst of life happening many times we find ourselves asking God, "Where are you?" Only to realize He not only is so close to us but He has been here before and has come back to walk through what He already knew was to come. Earlier I mentioned how I now know God was equipping me for this time, such as the conversation and dream I had a few short months before my life fell out from under me. I also know of other ways God was guiding and preparing my path in ways I thought were life choices.

In March (in the beginning craziness of the spring of 2020), I received a letter that a company had been trying to locate me since mid-January when I had been doing the not-so-pleasant task of sending out death certificates to everyone. Which seemed like everyone needed notification of Ted now being with Jesus because it is all I seemed to accomplish for the month of January. Anyway, this company's letter finally reached me with an urgent message stating "we need to talk to you now." So, with much drudgery I gave them a call. To my utter shock they told me that when Ted had purchased our Toyota Highlander in October 2017, he had taken out something called credit life (only on him) that if something happened to him the car would be paid off. What is so amazing about this is Ted never mentioned this to me and I don't know that he had ever done anything like that before when we purchased a car. I was always with him when we would buy a car except this one time when he did the transaction and I all did was go with him after the deal was done and signed my initials without knowing anything about the details of the purchase. So over two years before Ted went to walk with Jesus, God guided him for where I am now.

In the beginning of all the craziness of the spring of 2020 when the world was beginning to shut down and uncertainty was rolling in like it was the only option we had, I was reminded of these verses above. God goes before us so He is never surprised by the things of this world. Then He comes back and surrounds us with His presence to walk with us through the uncertainty this world tries to make us so aware of. Yet even in the uncertainty of this world He is faithful and trustworthy to never leave us or forsake us no matter what our path looks like He is always present guiding us into what He already knows.

Another way I now realize God went before me was the fall of 2018. I was teaching at Midland ISD and I was very discontent with teaching. (Imagine that that after thirty-five years of public education). One day, in frustration, I found where Midland Christian School is located and stopped by on my way back to our apartment and picked up an application. I went home filled it out and dropped it off the next day with my resume. There, at least I had done something to help my situation of being "done" with public education. See Ted and I had a plan to be in Midland until May of 2020 or 2021, and the obvious choice was for me to continue working to aid in our financial plan for retirement until we decided to begin living out our retirement. Even though I didn't really want to teach anymore yet still wanted the perks of summers off, two weeks at Christmas, a week at Thanksgiving and one in the spring I resigned myself to "welp, teaching it will probably have to be" since no other job I knew of offered the benefits mentioned. Maybe just "doing something" whether I heard from Midland Christian or not would help me be able make it through the two to three years I had left to survive in public education.

The end of April 2019, I got an email from the principal at MCS asking for an interview. Of course, I said yes and left the interview wishing I hadn't gone. Why? Because I really wanted to teach there! I told Ted, "If I taught there I could probably teach ten more years, babe, so you can keep doing what you are enjoying as long as you want!" Fast forward three weeks, and I finally got the call and they offered me a teaching position at MCS. After the weekend, I went in and told the superintendent that I couldn't take the job because I could only guarantee him one year because we had plans to leave the area in May of 2020. To which Mr. Lee replied, "We actually only offer positions on a year-to-year basis so that isn't a problem. When we were praying over the applicants, your name kept coming to mind for all of us. I believe God has something special for you here at Midland Christian."

Wow! So Ted and I went in a few days later to talk specifics of salary and what not. My heart sank when we finally got around to the mention of my salary. I tried my best to not show any type of reaction when the knowledge of taking a $15,000 cut to teach where I wanted to teach would be required (difference in public to private). We shook hands (remember being able to do that?) and Ted and I walked out the door telling the superintendent we would "pray" about it and I would let him know on Monday. We stood at our cars in the parking lot and I was like, "Well, bummer, there's no way we can take that kind of pay cut and still be where we desire to be by 2020." To which Ted replied, "We will be fine, babe. I think you are supposed to be here. It will be a great place for you. I agree the Lord has something special for you here."

On Monday, I accepted the position at MCS fully expecting to be there much longer than the one year that would bring us past our goal date of May 2020. Since I now I had a teaching position I could enjoy and Ted loved what he was doing out in West Texas we had already moved our "retirement" day back to May 2021. Why not? Life was going according to our plan. Little did we know that I was to be at MCS not so I could survive 2-5 more years of teaching but so that I would be surrounded by people who daily strengthened me in my walk with Christ. I was where I needed to be for where I am now. If I could have I would have continued to teach at MCS, but the Lord's plan was for me to be there for only a season of one school year even if it was disrupted by the events of the spring of 2020.

Yes, the Lord had something very special for me being at MCS, definitely not anything that I had considered but I was in a place where I was daily reminded of the goodness, faithfulness, trustworthiness, and love of our Heavenly Father. I was reminded daily how nothing surprises our Creator because He is already where we are going and doesn't just wait for us to get there but also walks with us every step of the way until we arrive. All the plans we had for the year 2020, have been derailed since December 31, 2019, and most of our wise retirement plan no longer an option. Yet I know the Lord has and is present in whatever is ahead because He has given me assurance of being there before I arrive while walking with me until I do. All because of His promise: "Have I not commanded you? Be strong and courageous. Do not be afraid; do not be discouraged, for the Lord your God will be with you wherever you go" (Joshua 1:9, NIV).

TIME TO BE UNCOMFORTABLY HONEST

Well, time to get uncomfortably honest. This is the first time I can recall being asked to walk through a life without being prepared. What does that even mean? I know my rambling thoughts are interesting to say the least. So here goes. I will try to explain: Life seems to take on somewhat of a pattern. (Yes, the analytical brain at work here.) Certain things can be expected. For most, life has guaranteed markers along the way. We begin school at a certain age, we move into the dreaded middle school time while looking forward to the freedom of high school and driving.

After what seems like an eternity, we finally turn eighteen, the age everyone has been warning us about and all the supposed responsibility that it brings. We begin preparing and expecting marriage, jobs, and children. Even though we are fully aware of the struggles of adulthood, we continue to plan, to prepare, for what we expect to come. As we age into our mid-thirties, we are in full swing of parenting and the fullness of "raising" our own children, we continue to prepare for the expected struggles we know that lay ahead with guiding children from ten to twenty-three into their own adulthood. We get it, we have watched, we have read, we have talked to others about their time when they were where we are. We prepare, we anticipate the highest probability of what is ahead so we can take it on in full force. If you are like me and are even further along the way, you have seen your parents age. They begin to need you more so you prepare knowing at some point you might have difficult decision to make for their well-being or even harder you can see their time with you is drawing near so once again you prepare for what is expected. You begin to brace yourself for what is the inevitable. Your parents will no longer be with you. You live in anticipation of the next expected marker in life. At some point along the way, you begin preparing for the magical time called retirement. You are working so you can be prepared to not work. You plan so wisely so the time you have left are those "golden" days so you don't have to spend your time bracing and preparing for what is ahead because that is now all behind you and you can just, well, relax and enjoy what each day brings because you have done all that in the past and now have walked into the part of life that you have been preparing for all the years before.

Well, all my preparedness didn't prepare me for where I am now. A lot of things have been on my radar throughout my life, and because of the way I think, I could tell where things were headed before they were even in front of me which allowed me to "prepare", "pray," "turn it over to GOD," whatever term we tend to call it in life that is part of us exercising our faith along life's way. Until now. I wasn't prepared for Ted getting to go walk with Jesus so soon. It wasn't on my radar. We had a plan a really good one for us both being alive and well when we both turned sixty-five. I still had a little over three years to get there. I was prepared for that, not this. These last nine months has caused me to think act and do in ways it never occurred to me I would have to. Ted and I had our plan be alive and well together in our "golden" retirement phase. I was not prepared to be figuring it out alone. He was the one who did all that. I didn't have to worry or think about it because he did.

He was prepared for our plan. I was just going to get to enjoy it. As I mentioned earlier about the question I thought was so fun and challenging to ask of others is now challenging me. If your life doesn't look like you thought for it to look, are you and Jesus still good? If I am being honest, the answer is yes. Jesus and I are still good. Not because I am some super amazing faith-filled follower of Christ who beats their chest and says, "Bring it, world! I will never question Jesus!" Not at all. Actually it is quite the opposite during this time I have realized God really does mean it when He tells us we just need faith the size of a mustard seed. I know now how little I bring to our relationship and how much Christ provides. He hasn't just met me where I am; He has picked me up and carried me from where I have been. I have only brought a broken, sin-leaning, self-indulgent, soul that has nothing to offer, and all I can bring is the forementioned as well as much more of this world that I have taken on. Jesus knows. He doesn't care. I am His, and He promises to never leave or forsake His children, and even as ugly as I am at this time in my life I am still His. He is faithful when I don't have faith. He is trustworthy when I can't be trusted. He loves when I am unlovable. He forgives when I am unforgivable. He brings His whole self into a relationship with His children. We don't have to bring anything because He gave everything so we can come to Him. Like Paul said in 2 Corinthians 12:9-11, "But he said to me, 'My grace is sufficient for you, for my power is made perfect in weakness.' Therefore, I will boast all the more gladly about my weaknesses, so that Christ's power may rest on me. That is why, for Christ's sake, I delight in weaknesses, in insults, in hardships, in persecutions, in difficulties. For when I am weak, then I am strong."

I now know how much through my life when I thought and proclaimed I was leaning on Christ to see me through I was depending just as much on myself and how good I was at preparing for what was to come. That is what all good analytical people do right? Head the situation off at the pass. Step in its way before it gets in yours. It worked for most my life, and I am sure Christ probably has had a lot of smile and nod moments (smile and nod moments are when words can't change what the one you are smiling and nodding at are thinking; they aren't ready to listen so one smiles and nods until the time is right and they are ready to hear what you have to say) with me as He has walked my life with me since I asked Him to be my Lord and Savior at eight years old.

    I don't mean to imply I didn't have faith in Christ or trust in Him for His presence because I did. I totally understood He is in control of all things. But because of my thought process I could reason and prepare for life to soften the blow. Which only means along the way I missed the opportunity to come to know the depth of His goodness, faithfulness, trustworthiness, and most amazingly His love earlier, which is what I have now realized since life brought something to me I was totally unprepared for. In my unpreparedness, I have found another level of God's goodness.

    I shared what I wrote above with a friend, and she responded with "Man! That's so, so good, Tam! I can totally relate to being the practical analytical mind that prepares for things, etc., and how you think you're relying on the Lord through it. But now have this season that deepened your dependence on Christ and you see how superficial or shallow your dependence really was compared to how much you relied on your own strength to get through things. I know this is true of me. Yes. So, when you 'get through this season' or 'figure it out'—I say that in quotes like do we really figure it out or officially make it—but when you find your footing, how will your walk with the Lord look different than it has in the past? Is that a question you know how to answer yet? Like how do you go about relying less on yourself when you think you've got it?"

To which my response was "because now I know. I didn't mean I had missed out or my relationship with Christ or it was any less then as it is now. But what I have come to know is the relationship I have with Christ I now realize isn't about what I bring to it but what HE does. He brings it all. And it is through His ALL that I am to live. His strength, His wisdom, His faithfulness, His trustworthiness, His Joy, His Peace, and His love. I now know something I thought I already knew. "Jesus replied, "You do not realize now what I am doing, but later you will understand" (John 13:7, NIV). Jesus said this to His disciples when He was washing their feet. I believe just like in Christ's relationship with the original twelve, He, in His relationship with us, walks along with us guiding us in ways we don't even recognize or do not yet understand until it is time for us to know, then we are able to know only because of the previous.

NOT SURE WHERE THIS IS GOING

I am not quite sure where to go now with my words. I know the thought "living behind the mask" will be explored. It just hasn't been given to me yet. In the meantime, I am beginning to come out of the fog and realize this is real. Unfortunately, because of the timing of the craziness of the world back in the spring and every part of life becoming dug up, I put on hold beginning to process the events of the last five days of 2019 and have been in survival mode—much like the whole world did because of the uncertainty it threw at us.

Now that we are at least out and about (masked up and backed up) and life has resumed somewhat of a normality my unexpected normal is setting in. All the different "stages" of grief can come in a day or a matter of minutes, and it is like a giant wave when you are close to the shore, and it covers you takes under and you find yourself further from the shore than a few moments before. I am learning to keep going toward the shore because that is where I need to be. Doesn't mean I won't find myself out in the waves in years to come but I know at some point I will be spending more time on the shore building sand castles than out in the waves. I am learning to not look too far into the days ahead and to just literally "take it one day at a time" which goes completely against my nature but not getting to far ahead keeps me from thinking on what I don't know yet.

I am beginning to live a little less prepared for my tomorrows and more in the presence of Christ which is where I have always been. I just realize it more deeply than before. "And why do you worry about clothes? See how the flowers of the field grow. They do not labor or spin. Yet I tell you that not even Solomon in all his splendor was dressed like one of these. If that is how God clothes the grass of the field, which is here today and tomorrow is thrown into the fire, will he not much more clothe you—you of little faith? So, do not worry, saying, 'What shall we eat?' or 'What shall we drink?' or 'What shall we wear?' For the pagans run after all these things, and your heavenly Father knows that you need them. But seek first his kingdom and his righteousness, and all these things will be given to you as well. Therefore, do not worry about tomorrow, for tomorrow will worry about itself. Each day has enough trouble of its own" (Matthew 6:28-34, NIV).

WHAT AM I TO DO WITH THAT?

One of the first things people said to me was "your faith is so strong it will get you through this," which sounds nice and encouraging, but it wasn't and I am still not quite sure what to do with that. Because right now it isn't about whether I have faith in Christ to get me through this because I do. Right now, it is about my life crumbling out from underneath me. I know God is good, faithful, and His faithfulness trustworthiness and love have been revealed to me on a much deeper level but it doesn't change the fact that I am having to figure out life in a way I had not planned or considered and in no way was I prepared to do.

Do I have faith God will guide me every step of the way? Absolutely. Do I trust Him to give me strength when I am weak? Of course, or I couldn't get out of bed every morning. My faith has not changed and is no different than it was before the last five days of 2019 not because of me but because of Christ, who is the same yesterday today and tomorrow. I know Christ has not changed just because my circumstances have changed. Unfortunately, my circumstances have changed, which means I have choices and decisions to make. Yes, I pray about them. Yes, I know the presence of the Lord is with me but it doesn't change the fact that I still have to make them I am still walking on a path that is different and unexpected. I have to figure out how to live without Ted in my every day. Yes, I have faith, most the time the size of a mustard seed but that is all the Lord said is asked.

Emotionally I have been strengthened and it has brought me through the last nine months, but it hasn't prevented what is required when life throws a curve ball and it seems life just whiffed the final pitch of the ninth inning to end the game. Decisions have to be made, adjustments have to come, facing the rest of my today's knowing they are not going to resemble anything close to what I am accustomed to or have been planning or preparing for is the reality ahead. Yes, faith in Christ will see me through and is the unmovable foundation I stand on but the changes are still ahead.

Faith doesn't change that. At least my faith doesn't change that, but Christ's faithfulness and His trustworthiness does. Because I have the promise that He will be with me through every choice every decision because He promises when I put my hope in Him I don't have to worry about what is to come. As His child, God has promised to care for me (Isaiah 46:4) and promises His children He will Never leave you or forget you (Deuteronomy 31:6).

LIVING BEHIND THE MASK

For ten years, while I taught in Chickasha, I had a sign on the wall that said, "Warning: my thoughts may become words." Several times students would ask, "Mrs. Williams, so what are you thinking?" To which I would always reply, "You don't want to know." It was quite fun to see them caught off guard by my response which by the way is a great classroom management tool never let high school kids see you sweat (remember that commercial from back in the day?). Don't let their behavior surprise, you even if you are so shocked it might take days for you to pick your jaw up off the ground—a.k.a. keep what you are really thinking behind your mask. With the practice I have gained over the years of teaching at the high school level, I quickly enacted the comfortable management tool of "living behind the mask." Hold my thoughts, hold my words because people don't really need to know what I am thinking. It isn't that I am concerned that someone might question my faith or I would disappoint them if I appeared to have less than they expected it is not that at all. It is just easier to smile and say, "I am adjusting," which seems to be good for others because they need to think I am doing well. I get it when a family member or friend is experiencing life in the way I have most have no clue how to help. Geeze neither do I, even after walking this path. I have learned most people are hurting for me and want so much to help me through this season I am in, but they just don't know how. I don't even know how to help myself because this is uncharted waters. They too are having to adjust to my new life and it helps them to know I am doing well

Honestly, with so many thoughts that are constantly going through my head, I am somewhat concerned what might come out, so my thoughts and words are masked to make sure others are not any more uncomfortable than they already are or need to be. I guess I began wearing a mask in January before it was cool (not really) later in 2020. It has been interesting to discover those who are more comfortable with the changes in my life and those who are not as comfortable yet. So for the time I continue to wear my mask and do my best to keep my thoughts to myself. Now there are days I think I need to find that old poster and carry it around giving fair notice to others "warning my thoughts may become words!" But for the most part, I haven't shocked too many with those times and for the most part I keep from sharing all the things that are going on between my ears. I am sure this doesn't sound healthy at all, but for me, it is working for now. It isn't that I am not talking to someone because I am always talking to the ONE—My Savior, my Rock, my Redeemer my Lord. The One who knows me better than I know myself. The One who was not surprised when Ted walked through heaven's gate.

"Your eyes saw my unformed body; all the days ordained for me were written in your book before one of them came to be."—Psalms 139:16 (NIV)

The One who promises to never leave or forsake His children is the One I am completely unmasked before. He knows when I am angry because I have told Him. He knows when I am sad because I have told Him. He knows when I don't think I can make one more decision or take another step because I just don't have anything left because I have told Him.

He knows everything because I have told Him and He has always listened. I know I am always heard. He holds true to His promise: "Come to me, all you who are weary and burdened, and I will give you rest. Take my yoke upon you and learn from me, for I am gentle and humble in heart, and you will find rest for your souls. For my yoke is easy and my burden is light" (Matthew 11:28-30, NIV)

THIS ISN'T IT

I constantly have to remind myself this world isn't it. We are created for eternity with Christ. So as much as I would love to claim Ted as mine, he never was mine He was always Christ's that is who Ted was created for.

The one perfect relationship that never fails, the one we all are actually created for. Being in this world is where we get the opportunity to come to know who Christ is. We get to choose Christ or this world. It is through our earthly relationships we are either pointed to Christ or we are pulled from Christ. I am so thankful Ted and I's relationship served its purpose. It brought both of us into a closer walk with our Lord and Savior. Through our imperfect individual lives, three beautiful lives were created and they too now know who Christ is and why they were given life, not for earthly gain but for eternity with the One who paid it all on the cross for any who will call on His name.

"For God so loved the world He sent His one and only Son that whosoever believes in Him shall not perish but have eternal life."—John 3:16

One of the first verses of God's Holy Word most hear early on in life explains why every person takes their first breath and until their last it is so they have the opportunity to know who Christ is for the eternity they were created for and to say yes to the free gift of eternity that is offered because of living in this fallen world. This world is unfair, this world is hard, this world hurts because it is fallen. But because of Christ we don't have to let the struggles of this fallen world hold us in its grip because being a child of God promises we are always held by the One who gave us our first breath and is there when we take our last and walk into eternity for which we are created. So as long as in this life we are pointed to why we are in this world, not for this world but for eternity, hopefully with Christ, then this world with all its trouble has served its purpose. My life with Ted served its purpose I came to know unconditional love, I came to know peace, I came to know joy, I came to know who I am truly am and why I took my first breath. I came to know Christ.

What follows is something from 2017, I think, which sums up what all my ramblings are trying to convey. I love you, Ted. I miss you more than words can even begin to express but more than anything thanks for always reminding me why we were blessed to be together.

What follows is pretty self-explanatory. I wrote it after a conversation Ted and I had on our way back to the apartment after church. Ted always had a way of helping my perspective with his snippets of wisdom. I shared this on Facebook on Sept 19, 2017, and lo and behold, it came back up as a memory Sept. 19, 2020. God's timing in all things always amazes me.

SEPTEMBER 19, 2017

"Do not let your heart be troubled. You believe in God; believe also in me. My Father's house has many rooms; If that were not so, would I have told you that I am going there to prepare a place for you? And if I go and prepare a place for you, I will come back and take you to be with me that you also may be where I am. You know the way to the place where I am going."—John 14:1-4 (NIV)

Since 2013, Ted and I have been on a quite a little adventure, and we have fondly named it our vagabond phase of life. In a little over four years we have lived in six different locations, three states, five jobs (between the two of us), sold and bought three houses, bought and traded in the neighborhood of five vehicles, all of which we have put literally thousands of miles on them as we have gallivanted across the middle United States. Now I must add, even before we started this phase, our desire has always been to live in Branson, Missouri. Branson is where we have wanted to call home. Well, this past week we took a step in that direction and closed on a condo in Branson on Lake Taneycomo! Woo Whoo! Now interesting enough, we have no clue when we will actually live in it as for the time we know we are to be in Midland, Texas, doing what we are doing. That info is shared so now I can get to the point of these thoughts. Sunday as we were leaving church Ted said, "You know when we went to Montana, that was a visit. When we lived in Borger, it was like we were just visiting, passing through as well. Then we lived in Amarillo and it too seemed like we were just visiting, and even now in Midland, it still seems like we are still just visiting and now we are going to end up in Branson and you know..." And of course, I had to finish his thought in my mind "we will finally be able to call some place home." But he so wisely finished with "we will still just be visiting because Branson won't be our home either because we won't be home until we are in eternity!" Wow! So wise and so true. Walk with Him! Be Blessed!

COMING TO A CLOSE

As 2020 is coming to a close, the date of Ted walking into the arms of Jesus is drawing closer. Like I have said, there are so many moments from December a year ago that are etched into my memory to this day a year later that sometimes my brain feels like it could explode when too many of them come flooding back—Ted waking me December 26, 2019, feeling my heart stop December 31, 2019, around 8:45 p.m. when he took his last breath, to planning His celebration of life, returning to Midland planning on finishing the schoolyear, life insurance issues, the pandemic exploding, deciding to move back Oklahoma, doing my best impersonation of figuring out which financial path to take, being blessed to find out Ted had taken out a thing called credit life when we bought the highlander (something he had never done before), which meant it was paid off, selling his pickup to an Oklahoma State Sigma Nu who was related to someone Ted worked with at the railroad, attending an Oklahoma State football game without Ted in his orange with his binoculars around his neck.

Pick a date in 2020 and I can probably tell you something from that day that impacted my life. It hasn't all been difficult. There has been joy and laughter through this year as well. A new granddaughter, Tallen Renee, was born in July. She is named after Ted Allen with my middle name. I have gotten to see more soccer games of our four-year-old grandson, Khyber. I have spent more time with our daughters since I am living closer. I have gotten to spend more time with our friends Becky and Phil. It has been amazing to get to talk with Becky as we both are going through life changes and as Becky said, "We are both in the same boat it just looks differently for each of us." My sisters have been, well, my sisters, like they always are. I couldn't have made it without them not just this year but any year of my life. They have helped me walk through 2020, a year much like no other, not just for me but for everyone.

SO...NOW WHAT?

Now that I have had to make decisions I had never considered having to make. Decisions I had no clue I was prepared to make. Have I made wise ones? Honestly, I don't know. I am making it where I am, financially, emotionally (most days), physically, I have adjusted to what is. So what do I know now that is different than the beginning of 2020? I have had the opportunity to walk in faith most the time the size of a mustard seed but my faith has never wavered. Not because I am some great person of faith but only because GOD can be taken at HIS Word. HE promises numerous times throughout HIS WORD to never leave or forsake His children. He said it so I believe it. I know HE has walked every step of 2020 with me just like HE had all the previous years of my life. HE has guided and been present through all these decisions I never planned on having to make. He has heard every word of anger, sadness, frustration, hopelessness even if it hasn't been verbalized. He has seen every tear, every frown, every thought and question that I have had in 2020. HE has not given me all the answers I have wanted but HE has been present. HE has never left me or forsaken me (walked away from me). Honestly, it still doesn't seem like I have much more "figured" out now than I did at the beginning of this year except I am now more assured that GOD is faithful and provides for HIS children, of which I am one, in all circumstances. Paul said in Philippians 1:13, "I can do all things through Christ who strengthens me."

I truly understand those verses now much deeper even When life doesn't look the way I want it to. My Savior is never wavering. He truly is the solid rock I stand on even if my life doesn't seem any more figured out the end of 2020 than it did at the beginning. I have always had faith in who CHRIST is, since I asked HIM to be my Lord and Savior of my life while watching a Billy Graham crusade on television as a third grader. I believe GOD is the creator and sustainer of Life. I also believe His Word and promises found in His Word.

When Faith and Beliefs are put into action it becomes Trust. Example (one I am sure you have heard) is a chair. I can believe a chair will hold me. I have faith in the construction of the chair to be strong enough to support me but only when I sit in the chair do I come to know the chair can be trusted to do what it is promises to do. Just like Christ only when our belief and faith in HIM is put into action do we come to trust Him.

One of my favorite songs growing up was "Trust and Obey." I think it went something like this: "Trust and Obey for there's no other way to be happy in Jesus but to trust and obey." Now I don't know what the writer of these lyrics means when it says "be happy" in Jesus. But if asked what I thought it means I would say there is no other way to come to know who Jesus is but to trust and obey. So again, what is different now at the end of 2020 than it was at the beginning of 2020? It doesn't seem like much is different on the outside appearance of my life but inward there is a very stark difference. 2020 has been the year of my beliefs and faith being put into action to grow my trust in CHRIST. I have surrendered having to know my next step (hard for a logistic mind to not go there, cause and affect run rampant in this brain of mine). That doesn't mean I don't have a plan, but it does mean I am learning to let go of having to know the whole plan. I don't have to figure out what is coming after what I know has run its course. I have come to know the Lord provides for me enough direction so I can go confidently in that direction yet only enough so I must remain in HIM and not run ahead.

Matthew 6: 25-34 says it like this: "That is why I tell you not to worry about everyday life—whether you have enough food and drink, or enough clothes to wear. Isn't life more than food, and your body more than clothing? Look at the birds. They don't plant or harvest or store food in barns, for your heavenly Father feeds them. And aren't you far more valuable to him than they are? Can all your worries add a single moment to your life? And why worry about your clothing? Look at the lilies of the field and how they grow. They don't work or make their clothing, yet Solomon in all his glory was not dressed as beautifully as they are. And if God cares so wonderfully for wildflowers that are here today and thrown into the fire tomorrow, he will certainly care for you. Why do you have so little faith? So, don't worry about these things, saying, 'What will we eat? What will we drink? What will we wear?' These things dominate the thoughts of unbelievers, but your heavenly Father already knows your needs. Seek the Kingdom of God above all else, and live righteously, and he will give you everything you need. So, don't worry about tomorrow, for tomorrow will bring its own worries. Today's trouble is enough for today."

Look at all the promises above that come together when it says, "These things dominate the thoughts of unbelievers, but your heavenly Father already knows all your needs. Seek the Kingdom of God above all else, and live righteously, and he will give you everything you need." If we seek/trust put into action our faith and belief we can walk daily with Christ knowing our needs will be met. The ones we don't even know we need and the ones we think we need will be removed so we can come to know how much more our Heavenly Father can be trusted. As we put faith and belief into action it turns into trust. Most importantly our trust is given to the ONE who is most trustworthy of all.

What is one good I can find in 2020? Through all the difficulty of this year, I have been given the unfortunate opportunity to learn to trust more in the One true God even when life doesn't look like I thought it would.

NO LONGER MY REFERENCE POINT

The Lord has healed my heart to be able to say the last week of December 2019 is no longer my reference point. I no longer look to it as my reason for decisions or choices. It is no longer why I live where I live or do what I do. HE, very gently over time, has brought me back to remembering my only reference point is the cross. The cross is the life-changing event where my life was given meaning, hope, and peace that can only be explained by what CHRIST did on the cross. If you are reading this because you happen upon it because life brought something like I have experienced into your life please know this: It is your own journey to walk. There is no right way, no timeline, no list to follow so that you will hurry up and feel normal again.

For the year of 2020, I was fragmented. It was as if my body, spirit, and mind were never in the same place at the same time. I did not know if I would ever feel whole again. But with GOD, all things are possible. He has loved me back to wholeness in the way that only HE can heal. Am I back to normal? No, because my normal (circumstances) has changed. But I am whole again. I have a hope for my todays.

I have permission to laugh, smile, and enjoy life like I always have. I expect goodness and my Saviors presence to be with me moment by moment in each day. Not because of me but because of HIM who is faithful and promises to never leave those He calls His own. Will HE do that for you? Yes, HE will, that is a promise He keeps. I can testify to that. I can't begin to tell you how it will look or what to expect but I do know He will be with you every step of the way. He is not surprised by where you are. He went before you and has come back to walk with you on this journey of unknown. I can testify to all the above. I have had the opportunity to experience His promises and His promises are true. To sum my ramblings up and what I hope has been made clear is my circumstances may have changed but Jesus Christ is the same yesterday, today, and forever (Hebrews 13:8). Even when your life doesn't look like you expected it to as you walk with HIM!

WHERE AM I NOW?

I asked a friend of mine, Anna, who lost her mother in the early part of 2019, to read what I have written. Knowing she had just experienced a life changing event similar to mine, I wanted to know her thoughts. If what I had written could possibly encourage others who are walking on paths different yet the same as ours. After reading it she suggested to me including a "where I am now" part.

So here goes: Where am I now? Do I still wake up most days and have to remind myself that Ted is no longer in my every day? Yes, but my response to those moments is much different than it once was. I no longer feel like a huge ocean wave has me and is pulling further out into deep unknown waters where I feel like may not survive. Instead, I am now reminded of all the mornings we woke up together encouraging each other for the day ahead and I am strengthened. Do I want to talk to him to know if decisions I am making are the ones we would make together? Yes, whereas once the desire to talk to him would make me feel lost and unsure, I am now reminded how we talked things out and I can almost hear the conversation we would be having about whatever it is I need to talk to him about. Do I struggle with allowing myself to be joyful, peaceful, and actually laugh a good part of my day? Yes, but I no longer allow myself to feel guilty for enjoying life even if Ted is not in my days. I am able to do that because of the way we shared life with a lot of laughter and joy and that is how he helped me to learn to live. Do I ever think a day will not be impacted by the week of December 26-31, 2019? No, because I really enjoyed and was blessed to share thirty-seven plus years with Ted. But I also know Christ has healed me so I could be reminded the last week of December 2019 is no longer and actually never was my reference point for the choices and decisions I make.

My reference point (like it really always has been) is the cross that is where Christ chose to take it upon Himself so just like me at the age of eight while watching a Billy Graham Crusade on television, everyone has the opportunity to hear the Gospel of Jesus Christ and accept Him as Lord and Savior. It is because of my reference point of the cross I have made it through this past year and I will continue to live and live well in Christ. As I have said before my circumstances have changed, my Savior has not. Jesus Christ is the same yesterday, today, and forever (Hebrews 13:8).

So where am I now? Walking with HIM! Being Blessed!

www.ingramcontent.com/pod-product-compliance
Lightning Source LLC
LaVergne TN
LVHW041550060526
838200LV00037B/1230